Temporary House

Temporary House

POEMS

CHRIS RANSICK

Middle Creek Publishing
Beulah, CO USA

Praise for Temporary House

Chris Ransick writes eloquently of the domestic and quotidian in *Temporary House*: fresh bread baking in the oven, a dog's love and loyalty, coaxing gardens through every season. *"Keep talking to winter as if / you had a tongue cold enough,"* he advises. In this posthumous collection, readers will find the poet's characteristic sagacity, as well as sardonic humor: Falstaff shuffling through Denver haunts; an epistolary to the high school reunion committee. Ransick's poetry continues to cast a rare light in the world. When he tells us, *"The next garden will be / as beautiful, you just / wait and see,"* we believe him—because we've learned to trust his singular voice, in all things poetic and beyond.

> — Joy Roulier Sawyer, author of Lifeguards and Tongues of Men and Angels

Temporary House is a powerful book. It captures Chris Ransick's muse in full cry, expressing where lifelong devotion to his art had brought him before the catastrophe of cancer struck. In much of this work Chris is a master symbolist. A mysterious and meaningful spiritual world shimmers behind or within our daily lives. As he addresses himself in the title poem, he is *"a bold dreamer / on a slow progress of myth after myth."* It is a world haunted by the possibility of hauntings, and where almost no discursive statements simplify or dispel that mystery, but rather *"words // keep rising in him like perfume."* Other poems, some of the strongest in the book and in Chris' entire oeuvre, are more dramatic, including the sorrowful "Watching the Eviction" and the slyly erotic and witty "Tax Shelter." Finally, as someone who knew and loved Chris, I am grateful to read—again and again—a poem like "A Morning Without Regret," where, within the tight structure of a villanelle, he says there is *"nothing to do I haven't done yet, / nothing I want that I haven't got. // ...What I owe my friends is my only debt."* I am grateful to know my beautifully haunted friend could imagine such happiness. That debt is paid.

> — David J. Rothman, author of My Brother's Keeper, Colorado Book Award Finalist; former Poet Laureate of Colorado's Western Slope; former Resident Poet of Colorado Public Radio

Chris Ransick was my good friend. I knew him in Colorado and on the Oregon coast, where we had both moved for personal reasons. I have never seen a poet grow by such leaps as Chris accomplished in the last two years of his short life, and these final books, *Temporary House* and *Joe the Ghost,* catch him at his best, darkly funny, humane, eager for life. He once told my students that poetry was the antidote to the mediocrity and dreck of ordinary life. His conversation was like that, like music, reaching into joy. I miss him terribly.

> — David Mason, former Colorado Poet Laureate, author of Ludlow: A Verse Novel

Temporary House by Chris Ransick is filled with precise and surprising language play. Playful titles such as "I Want to Disc with the Dalai Lama" are present along with serious poems such as "Watching the Eviction." There is a sympathy for the homeless, the abused, and a love and celebration of the natural world. These poems are highly imagistic and lyrical. Ransick masters the nuances of form and sound. These poems are packed with meaning and wisdom. For instance, he writes, *"It's easy to get permanence confused/ with mortality, and either with truth."* This is a gorgeous collection.

> — Sheryl Luna, author of Magnificent Errors, Seven, and Pity the Drowned Horses

Empathy and wisdom are hallmarks of Chris Ransick's poetry and nowhere is this more powerfully display than is his collection, *Temporary House*. From the rising scent of a newly seeded garden bed, or the soaring commentary of a raven in sky, to the broken wheel of a bicycle that has left behind by the abrupt flight of troubled neighbors, Chris examines a life, and finds every life—waiting for an acceptance, a landing, a home. I'll will read and re-read this book for years to come.

> —J Diego Frey, author of Umbrellas or Else and The Year the Eggs Cracked

For the kind ones—

you know who you are.

We cant even figure out how we got here.
But if we dont do it
Who will be cruel enough.

—Stan Rice

CONTENTS

Town Forgotten by Mountains

Here's the post office where each morning
I mail my dreams to insomniacs
and pick up replies, mostly hate mail,
but there are those few letters
that arrive, addressed in a frantic hand,
full of thanks and marriage proposals.

Here is the drug store where I
give blood. The clerk in his smock
among bottles and vials and so many pills
scoffs at my delicate wrists, at the whorls
my chin whiskers make, at my shabby shoes.

Here is the shoe store, closed.
Here is the barber who glories in
disjuncturing identity with haircuts
for which most refuse to pay. His shaves
open wounds, his only conversations
are of the haunting kind. His scissors
are dull as bigotry, his tonic smells of
grandfather's, he's missing an index finger.

Here is the afternoon rain, hallelujah,
and a white horse in a meadow,
black highlights on muzzle and loins,
ancient equine graceful tail that refuses to
cease against mosquitos. Riotous wildflowers
make sweet snacks after rich grass.
Here is the lake where the kids
no longer swim, their mothers'
fierce grip, fathers' sad faces.
The drowned girl was beautiful,
sun-browned skin and dark brown eyes,
voice that loosened honey from hives.
See how the low wall now

protects the shore, built from stones
people wept up on the beach.

Here, finally, is the nighttime hailstorm.
Percussion cut by dense, blunt thunder
surging subsiding surging. Crows long ago
huddled in low spruce boughs and
kept their remark to themselves. Who knows,
the river is already flowing madly among
the rocks and sings sorry chills all night,
a ghost flood no one sees, dry by dawn.

The Day He Counted Everything

He knew nothing of stellar
phenomena, but the curious
flash of a bolide breaking

yellow to orange to red, that
last night of August,
lighting the muscle

in him he'd ignored.
It was midnight. He named
the meteor zero, where all

numbering begins. Some hours
later, the glow before sunrise
made the horizon one, the sun

two. Every number a name
for how many, how much,
so his mind was three.

He ate a peach, his first food
of the day, but his fourth
object. The pit was five.

The crows were a gift
on the green expanse
and he counted each,

all the way to twelve.
The grass itself was no
matter till the sun shone

on a far hill, thirteen.
The woman in the blue car
frowned and the action,

not the emotion, fourteen.
This went on for some time.
The cumbersome numbers

finally weighed more
than the sum of their parts.
He tried to give them away,

to equate them, make them
speak, but they refused, multiplying
when he scolded their

divisiveness. Finally, he drew
minuses and they diminished.
He was back at page

one. There were two things
he needed to do and he couldn't
figure out which to do first.

Before I Bought the House
I Checked For Ghosts

I know about dust and so
looked there first for subtle
contrails plowing the surface,

faint boneprints in the plush
sifted skin sloughed by
people who fled their past.

I listened for sounds of
fists clenching behind
each door I closed, for

subaudible curses uttered
without breath, translating
language left after death.

In the empty bedroom, I caught
whiffs of earth and a woman's
perfume from the place

where the bed had been. Cold
caressed my neck and fine
hairs rose in response, flesh

at the roots tightening. Frost had
etched regret on glass where a ghost
pressed his banished face,

the window cracked where he
dry-licked the pane, aching for those
sliced mangoes on a blue plate.

Each key correctly clicked in its
lock and each time a soft shudder
spread concentrically, measuring

fragrant vacancy. In each room
I imagined furnishings and
each time, the room grew colder.

I turned to my friend and said
the place was imperfectly loved
and would do for us. Only then

did the elms loose old leaves
and the long icicles hung from
the split gutter spout

let their hoarded insults melt,
paused at the tip of each spike
every drip a soul's release.

Four Things To Do With A Dog and Time

1

Start simple, knowing he's
devoted and would go
to hell with you, to war
or to the thousand wars

and return. Any walk
will do. The columns
of the Parthenon hold no
particular mojo for dogs.

If he's a bird dog
give him room to run, quail
to flush from among
the gold hummocks.

Learn his exuberance,
which he gives away
free, as though it weren't
priceless. He has

less time than you,
probably. He knows all
your magic and secrets
and plays dumb.

2

Some dogs swim and
some dogs run so swiftly

down the green they light
small fires where their paws

strike the earth. Some dogs
will remember you for years

despite absences you could never
explain. Some dogs don't care

what you do for a living,
and will lick your hand

even if it smells of bad
decisions, poor drafts of

failed fiction, false
handshakes, hesitations.

Some dogs will follow you
down an Irish beach,

let you bury your face
in clean, sea scented

caramel fur. Some dogs
know all degrees of human

aloneness and can absorb
the dark blue hues.

Some dogs know before you do
what the poem is about.

3

Sit with your dog
on the day he dies. Run a hand down his flank.
Sing a slow blues song

Setting Free the Crow

He flies above you as you walk
up the frozen creek to the grave.

Once in a while you wave or speak
as if you could talk with his tongue.

Whose idea was this servitude and who
serves whom and is it always the same?

He seems to receive what you shed,
but you're not sure. He tends to leave

but a brief remark about all you unpack
from your heart, says the same if you

pack it back up. That's not code, it's
diplomacy, an offer to surrender

simultaneously and agree to meet
tomorrow, under a flag of truce.

Oxygen Man

Oxygen man, how could you know
how sad your blue truck looks from here?

The chilled liquid chills me as you
fill the steel canister at the curb

and I want to forget everything I know
about bones. Suddenly, the second hand

ticks louder, and I mean this literally.
The cat fears the cylinder's hiss,

so relentless it puts his to shame.
A white-rimed nozzle smokes beneath

thickening, scuppering clouds,
soon to sift a foot of spring snow

over the garden's bare, foolish beds.
Surely, someone understands I would

will her to live forever. I never had that
particular magic. The book of wisdom

is a rumor, the relics all imitations.
Forgetting is one man's wisdom,

witnessing another's, and the rest,
bereft, remember with lost words.

How to Teach Poets

You know enough to see you
know nothing. Your mentors

hang upside-down in the caves
where they wrote their poems,

their wisdom braided into
what you speak. You wish to

enforce no rules, but
can't always help yourself.

Some things clang and others
sing and words must serve

the reader. Go read the best
quirky ones who would not

behave and so show us
how to write. Open to every

poem, be clear in any praise
and kind enough for truth.

Write better poems
because you teach.

Enthusiasm is contagious.
Put feathers on your ideas,

release them into
any open country.

I Want to Disc With the Dalai Lama

The lost boys with whom I run
chain smoke and swear, thicken
the air with blunt desires. Jesters
and wise guys, gamesmen of rare
ignorance and good will,
they don't know Leonardo's line,
nor the love poems of Neruda.

Let me disc with the Dalai Lama at a
course hung with mists and moss,
where gentle gators return
discs to the banks unmarked.
How little a missed putt would mean
to the 14th Incarnation of the
Bodhisattva of Compassion.

I could finally learn to release
discs with mindfulness, master
secret techniques for speed
without effort, glide without
anxiety, landing where planned.
In my heart, only goodness.
In my ear, the laughter of

his holiness wading into thistles
in flowing orange robes.
True happiness, he'll say,
to find a bright disc in a field of
tall grass, a good line to the
chains, no detectable wind and
deepest quiet in the world.

Hot Wire

I named them the most
polite electricians—all

please and thanks and where
does the conduit go, Jack?

How much is slightly right?
Hey, buddy, I need help

with my pipe. Thank you!
They ate pizzas on my porch

and offered me a slice,
which I took, sitting among them

as they joked and licked sauce
from smudged fingers.

I was grounded by them,
as was my entire house.

They finished the job on time.
And the bill the bill the bill.

Watching the Eviction

The upthrust legs of the pink plastic chair
atop the sad heap of abandoned gear
draw my eyes from the text of King Lear.

I'd rather not watch the big-shouldered men
wrestling ruined mattresses stained with pain
up from the basement for their pocket of coin.

The ugly truth—I'm relieved to know
they're gone. The angry father had to go,
as did the sedated wife. The bobbing glow

of her cigarette at midnight in the alley
while she hosed down the lilacs with misery,
will nevermore steal my sleep. The valley

between my life and theirs was only crossed
by their neglected son who often tossed
rocks at my dog and was then nonplussed

when the animal charged the gate.
In dreams, it was the parents my dog ate,
and who then exploded his gut.

I used to give the boy peppers and beans
from my garden, hoping by some means
to nourish him with fruits and greens.

So I wince when I see his broken bike
pitched to the pile's peak. I would like
to go fix it since his dad went on strike

against fatherhood and preferred beer
and berating the boy, transferring fear
rom his life into the smallest thing near.

Where will they go? Will they wake
from self-inflicted descent and take
tools in their hands, a shovel and rake,

and get to work? How long will the mound
of abandoned belongings persist, a wound
wretched neighbors probe like a lost-and-found.

Will the boy ever be free, will he grow
wings? Somehow, I hope he will know
I forgive him all the rocks he threw

and every time he took the garbage out
I blessed him with poems, without
rancor, and flinched at his father's shout.

Falstaff on Colfax

1

He hits on the woman
serving his coffee in Pete's Cafe,
an awkward ghost in

clothes again and when
she laughs him off,
she laughs him off

honestly, which is rough.
He's not who he once was
and anyway, who was he?

He did have a horse,
a great roan beast retired
from fierce battles

and yes, the lovely server
would have been much impressed.
Later, he walks west, bars

blend into other bars,
The Ogden throbs and the
chicken joint's savory smoke

scents the sidewalk bazaar,
invitations in his right ear,
incessant traffic on his left.

2

Incessant traffic has left him
deaf in one ear, the effect of
walking away from the sun

mornings, toward it evenings
as it sets through a haze.
He sleeps to forget and fails,

reeking of spilled wine on a
raft of shade cast by a
smog-strangled juniper.

All he remembers when waking is
a dream-faded willow, how she
danced discarded beer cans

into the asphalt at the alley's
mouth, her spangled wrists
two graceful snakes

making whisper music
only snakes make. So what
if he sweats last night's liquors,

disgorges the dumpsterburger
as soon as he's choked it down.
This is how the discarded survive.

On the sidewalk, a wretched
half hard-on thumps his thigh
as he walks. Where's Doll Tearsheet

when you need her? Where
the bright garter given him
under moonlight and breezes?

A decent knight remembers
his pledge, how watchers on the
ramparts listened, envious,

as receding summer coaxed
the last scent from rows of
lavender spilling toward the river.

3

Lavender spills into the river
of pedestrians from the mystic
shop of crystals and incense,

its scent not enough to
mask the urine tang
infusing his vile apparel.

He still has his wits and knows
he's the cause of wit in others.
The briefcase containing

orders for his redemption
parades past, attached to an
unwhiskered whelp

whose gleaming black hair,
pomaded at great expense,
will soon enough molt

and expose the same dome
any man owns. One coin
in his pocket needs another

to jingle against and alone makes
neither noise nor sense
as a strategy for the war.

Better a thief than an utter
bore, better a grubby
lump of flesh than a seized

statue on a rearing horse,
pedestal bound at the center
of a traffic circle, pigeonshit

festooned and carbon-cloaked,
ignored by commuters
who never knew a sword.

4

He once knew a sword
was most powerful sheathed,
a threat implied, not uttered.

Now he slumps in the shade
of a doorway and shouts about
his anguish until sleep overcomes

his tongue. He wakes half sober,
which is close enough, and begins
again his quest for a butt of sack,

what's owed to any laureate,
to street spitters and tower sitters,
poets all who earn pain

one word at a time. His curses
are lyrics, but his bawdy songs
do nothing for the feral kitten

mewling from the folds of his
greasy coat, hungry as him.
Indian Summer can't last.

Soon enough, the wind will bite
beneath his rags and
every night will be dangerous.

5

Every knight is dangerous, even
an ancient one tottering
as he grubs gutter butts

and tucks them in a pocket,
not dry enough to light. He'll
still be damp come nightfall,

wretched and wine-dizzy,
half-starved, tucked in tight
against a reeking dumpster

and chasing dreams. Drunk
and listing past Kitty's,
he veers hard right, busts

his forehead on a pole.
Gears lock in his jaw,
but the pain stays distant

and his window-ghost's
bloodstain repaints in his
concussed, boozy brain a face

from lost soldiering days.
In that past was a message
he failed to write down,

though his ears ring with
fragments, eyes fill with the
full moon's flung sparks.

6

The full moon flings sparks
that settle and smolder on his
greasy coat as he sleeps,

curled into the iron angle
of a Cheesman Park bench,
dreaming of Eastcheap

streets, a fire roaring in the
Boar's Head hearth, tankards
of ale and bawdy songs,

when mocking honor was
easy, word-sparring and punning
with the prince of Denver.

Shivering Under A Blood Moon

I almost didn't rise,
4 a.m. October darkness a
poor trade for the perfume
and soft heat of her body
beside mine. The skies
had cleared and strange light
filled the bedroom,
lunar eclipse silvering leaves
outside the window,
then slowly turning their
autumn golds rusty.
Robe loose around me,
I stepped out into wet grass
and stood barefoot, shivering
as the ghost globe grew
red-edged, shadow at its
center, a luminous ring
locking for a moment the
circumference against
deep black space and stars.
And I let my robe fall away,
let the light breeze tighten
the skin on my back,
pale colors washing
the last garden fruits.

A Morning Without Regret

Dry snow deep as I forget,
bread in the oven, soup in the pot.
Bright winter morning without regret

and nothing to do I haven't done yet,
nothing I want that I haven't got.
Dry snow deep as I forget,

mandolin strings against ebony fret,
black coffee cooled with a whisky shot,
bright winter morning without regret.

Do what I must and take what I get.
Bury all hurry and should have and ought
under dry snow deep as I forget.

The fish forgives the fisherman's net.
The field forgives the parking lot.
Bright winter morning without regret.

What I owe my friends is my only debt.
Time's not a clock and can never be caught.
Dry snow deep as I forget,
bright winter morning without regret.

Slow Light

1.

Finally, it was forgetting
scared her most, her voice

trembling through digits
and microwaves.

She did not mind
being forgotten, but

that in dying you
surrender all memory.

2.

I saw so many crows
that autumn, drawing seams

around daylight from one
cottonwood to the next until

each hole in the dark
formed a star and a vast

dim smear of milk,
and the void, the mother.

Garage Haiku

January

frozen everything
blue air engulfs stone, glass, grass,
even my hand, writing

February

measuring arbor
desiccated vines rustle
without my hand's touch

March

peach buds swell early
false warmth gloves an iron frost
green gloves fisted blooms

April

survivors include
clematis, coreopsis,
weeds' pale fleshy roots

May

furious hail stops
suddenly, sunlight flares in
puddles of pulped leaves

June

ninety-eight degrees
hot wind whips mountains fires fierce
coreopsis blooms

July

capsaicin roils
scorpion's roots store blooming
leaves drunk on hot sun

August

bushel full of fruits
heavier than it should be
this year, 53

September

autumn morning chill
noon heat waits—which will prevail
breeze rattles beanpods

October

caterpillar curls
in spider's web, gold elms
were green trees before

November

all remaining vines
and stalks achieve final form
graceful agonies

December

white sun on the beds
snow smooth and subtly contoured
slow time on short days

Chop Wood, Carry Whisky

What good is a windy day? Trees
blow down and despite all that's sad
about that, there's the wood.

Chop wood, carry whisky, sit
by the fire and sail reveries
among the flames that never

settle. You can't fix what
isn't broken. The crow that
won't go is not mistaken.

If winter sunlight hits him right,
purple and green blush
along his neck. You've had years

to study his language and still
don't know the caw for
surrender, nor the crackle

of the fire that says take
another amber sip, let salt
sea over your lip and heather

under your tongue. Crow
gets none, though you both know
you'd be generous if he came.

Keep Talking to Winter

Keep talking to winter as if
you had a tongue cold enough.

Remember, wind never stops and
nights spill frost everywhere,

even into bones. Say
what you mean when speaking

to ice in the dark. Neither
has language nor hears.

Indifferent snow falls on both
high peaks and black gutters,

soon waters the same river.
Old winters gather in glaciers

and grow blue with history,
melt without intent releasing

and rinsing the Earth. Talk
to winter for your own sake.

Try to learn which way your
planet leans and write that

between lines, teach it to
crows, sing if you must.

Dead Professor

He's not dead
in the literal sense,
nor is his horse

lame. He dreams
at night like any man
of eternity, of

the clever students
and the others,
forever past and future.

He's planning his
final class. You bet your ass.
His work here is done.

He will take his books and
they will vacuum out
his office for, please,   *[sic]*

a kind, brave one.
He saved little bits
of love and thanks

in a drawer, aware
it was just to make
a small fire at last.

Temporary House

All refuge, an expanse of cool dark grass
in late afternoon on a sun-abused
summer day, all daily comes to pass.
It's easy to get permanence confused
with mortality, and either with truth.
You sleep your nights in a house, a bold dreamer
on a slow progress of myth after myth,
same repertory troupe, different drama.
The day you leave, by whatever means,
the indifferent weeds, the indifferent vine,
their mute ignorance is what remains,
wild herbs sprouting along a stubborn vein.
No haunting will happen, just memory
that shimmers down, itself temporary.

My Good Friend The Unknown

Consider this an open letter, one that
spills like the blue-black night sky

despite the stars, slows emptiness
between the trains that take us

home and far from home.
Fill time, spend time, watch it

come to rest as autumn sun on a
brave, shredded garden gone gold.

Wild bees know what it means and hurry
at the last white blooms on a lemon basil bush.

My good friend, why so shy? Reveal yourself
and the vacuum empties our fragile minds.

We're better off like bees with their burdens,
or the stars burning and burning out.

Your River Has a Beautiful Town

Bright trout among smooth rocks agree,
as do the dun and redheaded wrens.

Sunset on the current-rilled river
must be the star's best ritual.

Nomads and bar-haunters
kayak home under cottonwoods

and do not regret wind and whisky,
nor forget how a soft embrace

banishes the done day, transports
the traveler to well-deserved dreams.

Rough winter leaves as always
and exposes the brown hill has again

hidden its green intentions. What
can poor men and women do,

but find one another and insist
trouble be silent at night? This spring

same as the first and the last to come.
Even among cinders of the railyard

black-poisoned with industry, purple
will appear, yellow and white,

colors that can't stay, but come anyway.
Your river has a beautiful town so

sleep well as dark enfolds white peaks
and rocks slow-release their stored heat.

The Damaged Gentle Man

Slope of tough, fragrant sagebrush,
sunset lit, makes his weak valve
thrum and flutter. Words

keep rising in him like perfume
off those grey-green tufts,
and he vows to remember them.

If sunset lasts much longer
everyone there will be lost
in a reverie, and the wine

in their glasses will become the
best wine ever. The crows
may actually learn a new

note since they swoop
low enough to feel kinship
with the damaged gentle man.

His woman will make a map
of him tonight, careful to
recognize wilderness,

mark places where high chain
predators rule, not at all
sentimental, best left alone.

Magnetic Pantoum

Finally, it was the camera he noticed
above his face where he lay immobile,
a defaced effigy on a marble
sarcophagus, content with eternity,

ashy-faced where he lay immobile,
dreaming this poem into being in a
sarcophagus, content with eternity
but arguing with everything else.

Dreaming a poem into being in a
broken world, what choice is there,
but to argue with everything else
and ignore the alarms and banging?

Broken world, what choice is there
but to learn to bloom in decay,
to ignore the alarms and the banging
and step gracefully from the machine?

Learn to bloom in your decay.
The mind turns golden over time.
Step gracefully from the machine,
dress again in your common clothes,

a defaced effigy on a marble
frieze in a darkened museum wing.
Not even a camera would notice
the slightest smile on your face.

I Send Regrets, I Cannot Attend

I send regrets, I cannot attend
the 30-year reunion bash.
I hope the punch is fruity good,
the music nostalgic, but not so sad
that no one gets up to dance. Please
acknowledge the tunnel of despair
has narrowed for us all before asking
the next person, How have you been?

Don't smile your faces, either of them,
into fatigue. I forgive but have not
forgotten the insults in the hall, the
bad hair, the zits, the anguish.
Your invitation sits like a squished
plum in my hand, over-ripe and
oozing fermented juice. I extract
the convenient reply envelope and

slip this poem inside, careful to
fill out the return address to
indicate a far plain in Mongolia.
I hope the bald men you once dated
don't tilt you further toward truths
you've suppressed. I hope dead teachers
don't haunt the conversation. I hope
you finally manage to graduate.

Nine Reasons to Walk

Anything's better than this.
Maybe the long walk works.
The sun and the wind, yes.

The dog is staring
a hole in you and knows
you know. Give some joy

to him and it will circle
the globe and come back.
Think how your shadows

will ripple over the yellow
street. Bare trees tell
no lies. You will notice the

afternoon lasts longer. Walk
half as far as you want,
be happy walking home.

What a Father Tells a Daughter

Don't laugh because you may bear one yourself.
No script exists for coaxing nymphs from waves
to shore, nor one to tempt swarms back to hives.
To visit you, I swam across a gulf.
It was to love you that I learned to fly,
until the day you doubted I had wings.
I built your castle out of ancient songs,
a moat afloat with books, a tower high.
Each child's a mystery and time's too short
to waste in raveling out the stubborn knot.
I cut your cord the very day we met
and set you free because we're both that sort.
Now in your voice I hear a subtle chime
that marks the finest form I could become.

Thailand Black Tarantula

You stare at me alone in here
and think me delicate,
though I visper vicious words.
My anger and my wit

are poisonous, just like the tear
I'd open in your palm.
I'm agile, I'll become a blur
just when you think I'm calm

and I'll leap toward your throat,
whose pulsing calls to me.
The bite won't kill, all pain is thrill,
so come and set me free.

Poem for My Students #2

At one point, your tattoos began to animate
like Bradbury's illustrated man, colors
swimming, lines ashimmer as though
deciphering codes. Some nights
I have tried to imagine a silver
tongue in my mouth struggling with
phuopsis or singing the ancient songs of a
Persian mystic. I've crossed muddy
mountain passes with you, been trapped in
filthy motel rooms with hookers and
heroin addicts. I've eaten pecan pie under
magnolia blossoms in a town that forgot
its manners. The guns in your stories never
actually shot their bullets, but
they might yet past those swabbing
puddled urine from tiles or restraining
a crazed man. My job is easy, paper and pen,
plots and subplots, prognostication,
sharpening blunt lines to fine points.
I would not have you study
chemistry, but rather the chemical
reactions in scenes where touch
is withheld from a woman by a man.
Let the cyclists zip down French streets
while you munch a sausage. Let dreams of
empty rooms signal the coming of light
through the clouds to banish pain.

Four Poems for Bees

1

Give me a hundred
worker bees, a few drones
to serve their queen.

Give me hard noon sun
on brick. Give me a little
luck. Give me a break.

Give me a loyal dog
who does not recognize
degrees, only kind

companionship as the
measure of a man.
So my prayer is

give me these things
I already have, the good life.
Oh, and that swallowtail, too.

2

Pennyroyal bush of
pale purple blooms,
stems tremble when a
hovering bee lands
at a blossom and
finding no nectar
flits up instantly, seeks
another in the poison mint's
proliferate leaves.

Green-chromed sweat bees,
wild with hunger,
barely bend stalks.
A fat black bumble with
swollen pollen sacs
makes a thin stem dip
where she hangs to rest,
face plunged in shade.
Above, a tough vine
dangles sleek, pendulous
cucumbers whose tendrils
tend to grow all night
even as our dreams
teach us to climb.

3

Winterbee, emerging early,
late winter noon's hot sun

on the hive, on my house,
has fooled us both. Regret

is of no use against February
and the frost coming tonight.

If only you'd been patient,
I could have offered larkspur

so sweet, warm perfumes rising
off splayed valerian and

sticky white tobacco flutes.
You'll never hover there.

I could have given you a
heaven of corn, an aerodrome

alive with winged ones. I close the
greenhouse door against cold,

but you've followed, scenting alyssum
that blossomed this morning, even as

snowbanks melted, and how you sail
delirious, over sprouting marigolds,

a frail balsam apple vine, before
folding your wings and keeling

in among rattle gourd sprouts,
making a beautiful death.

       4

The man who wastes time
in gardens will not have to plan

his joy. Blue flowers spring
from his tongue and every

crow knows not to worry at his
proximity. He will pass hours
creatively, and also rest, hands
in his lap and eyes closed,

focused on aromas, breezes
intending to be fascinated.

He doesn't collect, he inhabits,
as the dog in the shade

understands, as does
every bee in the sun.

My Loyal Friend

He hunts like any hungry
dog, prefers rabbit to squirrel,

but hey, takes what he gets.
The fierce bark, the teeth

are no real threat unless you
smell strongly of lies, acts

you remember, but must deny.
You know the forest well enough

and can have a head start. Run
down from treeline into pines,

pray if you think it will help, make
promises and deals. He'll be

on your heels. He knows neither
kindness nor your crimes.

Message to the Gods

We want to do it by ourselves with these
skinny bodies and toughened hands, with our
cloths wrapped round us against the cold,
with our fancy voices, with our bold brains.

But wind wind wind stiffens us,
makes our eyes water and our throats ache.
Again the grain harvest is very poor
and our babies die, the weak ones among us,

the lingering old. Bitter winter
blows rain aslant through the thatch and we
starve beside lovers and friends. Frozen sod
won't yield so we burn their bones to ash

and let it drift in gusts across stubble fields.
We would do your will if only you tell us
what it is. We scour our souls to find
little bits of evil and cut away that flesh.

We lie, faces pressed to hoarfrosted
weeds. We drowned a virgin, which only
made things worse. We carved a great horse
into the hillside. We built you a house.

What else? At dusk, you laugh thunder
and at dawn, your misted breath settles
in the folded valley, but only the mad ones
claim they have glimpsed your faces.

If your one gift is death, give it to us
all at once. We are ready. We stand among
bare trees, leaning into one another, mouths
ready to receive your kiss of disease.

Reoriented by the Drunkard

I'd lost patience with his stumbling,
his shiny eyes and smears of language,

an embarrassment of a man trapped
by gravity, teased by December trees,

whipped by freezing wind.
How far I have fallen to keep

such companions, I who am so
sure of my own steps, my

destinations, always anxious to arrive.
Just then he stopped, drew back

his shoulders, squinted into low
winter sun and said, I know

I'm a shambling mess, but will you
just look at the blue of the sky.

Tax Shelter

Woman, let me be your tax shelter.
When you have calculated
down to the last dime what you owe,
come to me and we will open our
thick, steely vault to reveal a jewel.

Or better yet, calculate upon me,
on the freckled skin between my
shoulder blades. Cipher away, scribe
equations up and down my spine
until you find the bottom line, baby.

I will be your magic accountant,
I'll seek and find your secret stash
and for a fee line up innocuous
columns of lies so the numerals
mount toward equilibrium and tip

into emptiness. Yes, I can do this
and so much more. I can run my
big exemption into the heart of your
income. I can rumple your sheets
so even the auditor must look away.

After all, we've got all night to
make these elegant figures balance.
Give me your receipts, both of them.
Let's have a look at that W2.
I'll lick the envelope. Here's a stamp.

How the Falcon Forgets

Here in the land of little sleep,
good men speak with lips aflame,
calling themselves by a different name
down in the fiery deep.

What if you woke and had turned to stone,
monolith above a gray-green bay,
wind to wear you smooth by day,
and moonlight to bleach your ruin?

Wave is indifferent to the shore it wets.
Buzzard abandons the bone she flenses.
Rain falls the same on windows as faces.
Flight is how the falcon forgets.

Never fell the old hawthorn tree,
the mad one scratching at distant stars.
Think of the hills as rocky piers,
set the rioting grasses free.

Swim down the river until you reach
the bend where the water grows still.
Float the rapid and the quivering rill,
wash up in the shade on a sandy beach.

Here before dawn you may finally rest.
All night long the water grows deeper.
Once you fall in you're a heavy sleeper,
heart so slow in your chest.

Directions for Writing Your Own Epitaph

Write your name and then
erase it. Invent a new word

that sums up your life and
use it in a sentence. Attach

date of birth and describe
the weather on that day,

whether flying snow sneaked
under doorsills, drifted over

the hood of the car. How many
magpies and crows did it take

before you broke the code,
caws and pauses, pauses and caws?

There's not enough room
on the stone they chose

for your whole story so
make it a poem, break lines

at the musical joints so they
sing as chiseled in stone.

Epitaphs last, but not
forever, so whatever you name

will slowly be smoothed away
by the moon's reflected light.

The Gentle Hands of the Dental Hygienist

Prone under brilliant lights,
I expose the bone geometry
of my flaws, oddly angled
jawsprouts, the pink cave
where filtered thoughts queue,
awaiting expression. She leans
in, masked face hovering inches
from my own, breeze from the AC
nudging blonde bangs, long lashes
flicking over hazel-green eyes.
When her breast presses my
shoulder I deep-breathe her scent,
both of us silently accepting our
portion of a necessary intimacy.
Strong hands under pale blue latex
grip the steel pike, pinky braced on
on my lower jaw, forefinger
lifting my fleshy upper lip as she
probes under sensitive gumlines.
Then comes the familiar series of
small sharp pains, again, again,
copper infusing the mint aroma,
tools singing through tooth enamel
to the inner ear, of fierce gentleness,
touch that belongs to lovers and healers,
those we trust, to whom we submit,
lying back, mouth open, eyes closed.

Garden Haunt

1

Wet flagstones and moonlight, snails
for friends and none too many, but
better than not having any. What
do you name their glowing trails?
Like them, you hide in plain sight.

You take the living for fools,
their elaborate schemes, the cultivated
food forest that in sun, articulated,
fruits in bright shapes, waterfalls
until deep frost-truncated.

Yet like the living, in the audience
for the frantic crickets' crosscut song,
August slows on a failing wing.
All haunting is subservience
to night with no awakening.

2

Awakening at night, subservient
to a crescent tucked in a cloud,
you recite all your sins aloud.
The unripe melon luminescent,
dank vines a bad neighborhood.

It had to be one or another plot,
so why not this, with its obscene
squash, the purple insane
crenellated kale, as good a spot
as any. Moonlight, damascene

on spatulate leaves, is art
you alone appreciate. Hover
in the corn, in coreopsis quiver,
fade from the garden's heart
at red dawn, that late arriver.

3

Red dawn arrives at garden's heart
a little late, everything tilting.
Even shadows mimic wilting
where stalks endure, so hail-hurt
they seemed to be melting

into soil. Given just one chance,
all of us live by recovery,
morning always a discovery.
The last ghost used to wince,
reduced to petty thievery

and mumbling by the compost.
At least hoist a rake and shovel.
Eternity takes a while to ravel,
longer than forever, almost.
Reap every aphid and weevil.

4

Reaper, every aphid and weevil eats
leaves and leaves rude waste.
You appreciate their taste,
though nightly, regret accretes
with each breeze lifting a mist

off scented herbs, lavender and mint.
You thought to hide in the hops
pale, soft cones heavy hung at the tops
of tall vines, rasp useless against ghost skin.
What poetry was on your lips?

What did you whisper to the corn
when the moon was large? Crow
won't reveal what you'll never know.
Previously invisible, you emerge reborn,
lupulin dusting you like gold snow.

Poem for the Couple Who Walk
Down My Street Every Day

Side by side, stride for stride, not
holding hands, silent.

At 3 o'clock sharp I look
and they're always there, briskly

heading south toward the park,
he in a floppy hat, she in a hood,

so I've never seen their faces.
I know they are old, if measured

in years, young in the speed
and purpose with which they walk.

Every time, I want to
follow. Once, I grabbed my shoes

and laced them, stepped out
in the light rain only to find

they were gone beyond view.
Some day, I may lie in wait

and invite them to share coffee
and tell me their names, the names

of their children, the story
of the day they met, the secret

of making a walk into a
ritual, the simple magic

companionship offers anyone
daring enough to accept it.

Your Auburn Hair, Along the Seine

It billows inside the frame
upon my shelf, your auburn hair

along the Seine, in Paris, several
years ago. You were not young,

but younger than now,
stepping through March frost

on your way to work. I've known
your happiness as a warm

green river, your sorrows as
riverbanks and clouds,

and all of it I'd know again
from the beginning.

Empty House Left to Crow

1

Consider it a gift, a hollow gesture
where emptiness signifies respect.

Finally clear the layers of language
within caws repeating for years

in the canopy. When magpies came
in gangs and raided the corn, you

rasped way back in your throat,
beaked argo of a patient inquisitor,

a song twisted with indifference.
The house is yours though you have

never read one of these poems.
You'll miss our conversations

when you taunt the dull neighbor
in your boredom and are ignored.

2

Love the bird from below, the worm
from above, the wind from within.
Under this roof, watch the hailstorm
comment on the garden again, again.
Lucky to seek and to find,
lucky to end what you began.

3

Dents prove memories,
the wild fastball high and
outside that ticked the
top of the mitt, the fencepost,
and dimpled the garage door.
Remember the neighbor girl,
once small enough to
sit in the swing, hauling
heavy bags to a waiting
van, her father's glare,
over his shoulder the
ghost of a woman who
haunts the alley, weeping.

4

Crows chortle at the
magpie funeral,

rasp low snide remarks
from bare ash branches.

What were her chances
against a fast hungry fox?

The raucous calls,

vortex over a
torn tuxedoed corpse,

are operatic, a collective
defiance, memory making.

All this amuses those
onyx conspecifics whose

scolds make a knot of
sympathy and contempt.

5

November snow will collapse the greenhouse.
Cheeseweed will win, and crabgrass dance
over every barrier, setting fierce roots
in choice soil. Snowmelt will puddle in
specific places, black ice retreating as
sun angles back the garage shadow
incrementally per day, proof of planetary
motion. At noon, heat will pause
and spill itself everywhere, coaxed
away finally by lengthening shade.
Crow can have whatever remains,
husk, pod, seedhead, cricketsongs
as accompaniment, long stretches
of elaborate silence. The elms won't live
forever and will have to come down
in pieces. Imagine the old wild roses
free to show their harbored intentions,
filling the nook with barbed spines.
Let any beetle or worm reign, let a jungle
assert itself under rank vines, rope tough.
Crow can be sheriff, with a host of black
deputies, cronies if there ever were,
each a murderer in a collective
innocent of our law, keeping its own.

6

The house will echo, nothing
can be done about that.

Also, the walls. They've absorbed
joys and just enough

despair to prove the pain.
The blue woman is my mother,

transparent and trust me, gentle.
Crow has observed, knows the

garden well, will call out names
of plants and in general

supervise. Take little of it
to heart, but remember that

dark bird's tone and repeat
as needed, a nihilist's laugh

mixed with good advice and
salted with accusations.

The Next Garden

The next garden will be
as beautiful, you just

wait and see, though around
its perimeter different boughs

will hang and different vines
will grip and twist into new

sigils. How much rain
will fall? Thunderstorms or

Pacific mists, an ocean of
snow or limitless fog?

First, learn how Earth turns
in that particular place.

Observe different birds,
discover new soil and then

the many bugs. Gardens
comprise a microcosmos

a human imagines
and inhabits, steward

who cannot stay long.
Bring all the tools you need,

pencil and paper,
eraser, eraser,

spade, rake, and bucket,
memory of tendrils,

back full of muscles,
bench for a shaded alcove.

New Oath

1

Know you are a wild man
emerging from a dark grove
stunned and hungry, blinking in
sunlight. Shapeshifter, choose
first the fox for night and earth,
then crow for sky and day.
Go to ground or take flight, but find
where the rains fall on the vineyard.

2

Wind lets the crow forget
and you can learn by watching
what wings make of it. Moonlight
hides the fox in a silver blur
so he owns the dark field.

3

The sunlight's good, the soil
black and deep in the meadow.
A creek marks the far edge, crisp
cold watercress and brookies,
fed by a feeder springs.
All morning, light floods the field
and by evening shadows blend
to dimmer silhouettes.
Sometimes music sifts
from the forest, always a descant
to the birdcall and breezes.

There's a writing desk and stove
in the small cabin near the water.
Stay as long as you like.

ACKNOWLEDGMENTS

Middle Creek Publishing and the executors of Chris Ransick's estate sincerely acknowledge that some of the poems in this collection may have been previously published in journals, magazines or anthologies, in print or online, but that we haven't record of that.

If there are acknowledgments of such known to any reader, we would humbly request that someone please contact Middle Creek Publishing that we may get those acknowledgments into subsequently issued copies of this title.

Special gratitude to Lighthouse Writers Workshop for the impetus and generosity in the acquiring and release of this book.

Gratitude to the Denver literary community, and Chris Ransick's fans and readers from the region and beyond.

ABOUT THE AUTHOR

Chris Ransick, Denver Poet Laureate from 2006-2010, was an award winning author of six books of poetry and fiction. He was born and raised in upstate New York and lived in Colorado, Montana, Wyoming, California, and Oregon. He worked as a journalist, editor, professor, and speaker and served on his city's public library board, his state's humanities board of directors, and on the PEN Freedom to Write Committee. His first book, Never Summer, won a 2003 Colorado Book Award for Poetry. His book of short stories, A Return to Emptiness, was a 2005 Colorado Book Award for fiction finalist. His stories and poems have been presented on television, radio, and stage, including collaborations with Ballet Nouveau Colorado. He was a faculty member from 2005-2019 at Lighthouse Writers Workshop, Denver's independent creative writing school. Lighthouse awarded him the 2013 Beacon Award for Teaching Excellence. Chris held his final reading at Lighthouse Writers Workshop on September 25, 2019.

Middle Creek

Publishing

ABOUT MIDDLE CREEK PUBLISHING

Middle Creek Publishing & Audio believes strongly that responding to the world through art & literature — and sharing that response — is a vital part of being an artist.

Middle Creek Publishing & Audio is a company seeking to make the world a better place through both the means and ends of publishing. We are publishers of quality literature in any genre from authors and artists, both seasoned and as-yet undervalued, with a great interest in works which may be considered to be, illuminate or embody any aspect of contemplative Human Ecology, defined as the relationship between humans and their natural, social, and built environments.

Middle Creek Publishing & Audio's particular interest in Human Ecology, is meant to clarify an aspect of the quality in the works we will consider for publication, and is meant as a guide to those considering submitting work to us. Our interest is in publishing works illuminating the Human experience through words, story or other content that connects us to each other, our environment, our history and our potential deeply and more consciously.